My Caste-My Shadow
Selected Poems

"Turn in any direction you like, caste is the monster that crosses your path."

—B.R. Ambedkar

By the same author

Fiction

The Stricken Moth (1984) Writers' Workshop, Kolkata

Alone in the Wilderness (2000), Writers' Workshop, Kolkata

'*She's Black*' '*Glass Walls: Stories of Tolerance and Intolerance from the Indian Subcontinent and Australia*' Orient BlackSwan, 2019

Translations from Punjabi

A Season of Nights, Puran Singh Kanwar, National Book Shop, Delhi, 2006

Pash: A Poet of Impossible Dreams, Pash Memorial International Trust and Shilalekh, Delhi, 2010

Lal Singh Dil: Selected Poems–Exclusion Deprivation Nothingness, LG Publishers Distributors, Delhi, 2017

Translation from Hindi

Premchand: God's Share in Stale Rice and Other Stories, LG Publishers Distributors, Delhi, 2019

Non-fiction

Pattern and Significance in the Novels of R.K. Narayan, Indian Literature, Sahitya Akademi, 1975

Learning a Foreign Language: Gulliver's Way, *FORTELL* (Journal of Teaching English Language and Literature), published by Forum of Teachers of English Language and Literature, New Delhi, January 2012

Reflections on having been a Learner before becoming a Teacher of English, *Language and Language Teaching* (Azim Premji University) Volume 4, Number 4, Issue 7, January 2015

Translating Punjabi Poetry: An Approach, *Language and Language Teaching* (Azim Premji University), Volume 6, Number 2, Issue 12, July 2017

My Caste-My Shadow
Selected Poems

Balbir Madhopuri

Translated from Punjabi by

T.C. Ghai

First Published 2020

ISBN 978-93-83723-70-6

Published by
LG PUBLISHERS DISTRIBUTORS
49, Street No. 14, Pratap Nagar,
Mayur Vihar Phase I, Delhi 110 091
Email: lgpdist@gmail.com

Laser Typeset at
Sakshi Computers, Delhi

Printed at
Sapra Brothers, Noida

Contents

Introduction

Balbir Madhopuri is a renowned signature in the world of Punjabi letters. He began his literary journey as a poet but he has excelled in prose as well. So much so that his autobiography *Changiya Rukh* (The Lopped-off Tree) has been published in translation in several languages including English titled *Against the Night* published by the Oxford University Press (2010).

The present volume is an anthology of his poems selected and translated from his collection *Meri Chonvi Kavita* (My Selected Poetry) (2011), which was dedicated to the memory of the Punjabi Dalit revolutionary Mangu Ram Mugowal (1886-1980)[1], and opened with the poem *Begumpura* (City of No-Sorrows) by one of the most revered medieval Bhakti poets, Ravidas (1450?-1520?) of Kashi (Benaras) belonging to the leather-working community, who forcefully challenged Brahmanism like the iconoclast Kabir. *Begumpura*[2] is one of the 40 compositions of Ravi Das included in the Guru Granth Sahib, the sacred text of the Sikh religion. These two gestures to the Dalit heritage well locate Balbir Madhopuri in the ideological trajectory of India.

Madhopuri's poetry is the product of his deep sensitivity and enhanced sensibility. It is best expressed in his own view about literature:

> This (Dalit) literature is not just a means of entertainment or killing time. It prioritizes an ideological and a socio-economic revolution and cultural change. A writer nowadays doesn't submissively shy away from portraying the harsh and cruel social order. He continually attacks the hypocritical, dubious, devious and ritualistic culture of the society with his rational word-missiles. The result is the emergence of a different India within the older elitist construct. Plural India with multiple cultures, languages and religions has received a sharper relief in the past few years. Literature has become multi-vocal with different cultural expressions. Indian literature can no longer be measured with a single yardstick. The need for different aesthetics has long been felt. Dalit literature, in this context, is the expression of a humanistic ideology seeking a revolutionary social change based on equality, fraternity and justice. (translated from Madhopuri's introduction to *Meri Chonvi Kavita* (My Selected Poetry, 2011)

Madhopuri divides his poetic journey into three stages. The first was that of his early school and college level romantic poetry that he has left behind. In the next stage his poetry is embedded in the troubled days of Sikh militancy of 1980s of which he himself was a victim. His moving from Punjab to Delhi in 1987 was a great relief that helped emboldening his poetic reflections. Humanistic and progressive vision is reflected in his first anthology *Maruthal da Birkh* (The Desert Tree, 1992).

Madhopuri says the third stage of his poetry began when he consciously started composing from 'the purely Dalit revolutionary perspective'. This was facilitated by his residence in the cosmopolitan Delhi where he read Dalit literature from other vernaculars and increasingly interacted with Dalit litterateurs. His earlier grounding in the realism of Soviet literature awakened his Dalitness in a major way. All this is best manifest in his anthology *Bhakhda Patal* (Smouldering Underworld, 1998). He reflects: 'I feel my poetry expands the social consciousness of my ancestors, my elders. It has assumed a permanent form of that heritage. The only difference is that it is now a cerebral rather than merely a physical struggle. It ignites the light of consciousness among the people who have lost their land, wealth and religion.'

The first four poems in the present anthology offer what poetry means to Madhopuri.

In *Poetry Is Not Mere Words*, he asserts:

Poetry is not mere words.
It is
the flight of a man
without wings.

Poetry is not mere words.
It's the agonizing cry
of a black partridge
snapped up by a falcon
as it flies out of a sugarcane field.
It's the frenzied outcry
of a deer terrified in the wild;
the story of leaves
precariously dangling
from the branch of a tree.

Madhopuri seeks and is proud of the distinct flavour of his poetry. In *A Wish for My Poetry* he says:

I don't want
my poems
to fall into a river
like monsoon nullahs
and lose their identity.

I don't want
my poems

to become part of the poetry-stream
whose scriptures
divide a vast field
into small enclaves
and reserve the velvety greenness of grass
for those on top of the pyramid;
to forbid dark-skinned people like me
to open their third eye.

Even though Madhopuri burns inside, his poetry becomes a calm expression of his understanding. It is best reflected in *My Caste*:

My caste is always with me
like my complexion
like my shadow.
We are so rolled into one
I'm nothing
except my caste,
wherever I am
in the city or in the village
here or across the seas.

Madhopuri has a clear idea about the deep-rooted nature of the hierarchical Indian social order and the deep-seated prejudices of the oppressive castes towards Dalits and Adivasis. In *Sanskriti* he laments how even in the fast-changing world, the frozen mentality of caste Hindus is not ready to change its attitude. Dalits are forced to feel low. The poem *A Man Lighter than Straw* epitomizes the generality of the situation:

Quite often
this clayey body
becomes thinner than water;

words
desert the tongue
like leaves fallen from a tree
in autumn, and
I feel I am drowning
and the earth does not open up to swallow me
when suddenly
someone wants to know
my caste.

Despite all kinds of discrimination he has suffered and the humiliations he has borne, Madhopuri never becomes cynical. He has faced all challenges bravely and has retained the core value of love, compassion, and understanding. His gratitude to his relatives and friends is abundantly reflected in his poetry. He pays a glowing tribute to his wife in *My Life*:

Ever since she has stood beside me
we are one-and-one eleven.
My feet sail above the ground.
I have left far behind
the jungle of deep sorrows,
piles of hatred.
I have laid down before her love
weapons of anger-resentments,
of animosities.

Madhopuri doesn't suffer from any caste animosity even if he had to be the butt of the same. *An Oasis* is a poem dedicated to his brahmin friend Purshottum Sharma:

At times
he is distant like the sun
and close like the sunshine

Sometimes he is brilliant sunshine
sometimes an umbrella
sometimes a protective sword
sometimes the Lakshman Rekha

During a drought
he is a dew drop
In the desert
he is an oasis

How does one locate Balbir Madhopuri's radical poetry? How does one understand his resilience, his power to subject his surroundings to a critical scrutiny to weave a social order full of love, compassion and understanding? Is it his individual enterprise? Or is it what he partakes from his heritage, howsoever hidden and opaque it could have been? One must identify its deeper roots. First of all, it is in the nature of ever-changing Punjab from where he draws his intellectual sustenance. Punjab formed the north-western frontier to the Indian subcontinent where people from across Afghanistan would first move to while coming to India. It was subjected to all kinds of inflows; from invaders to merchants, from warriors to artisans, from religious scholars to folk singers and dancers. This multifarious influx made people living in Punjab to be warriors but also accommodative to new arrivals, whether people, their wares, life styles and ideas. Nothing could stay unchanged in Punjab due to its geographical location. If Aryans invaded Punjab and in the due process composed their Vedas here, they couldn't withstand further pressures from the north-west and the Buddhist ideas and practices got rooted here, hugely disturbing the Brahmanical divisive ideas and pushing them towards east. The egalitarian ideas and practices survived the decline of Buddhism in Nath Yogis and Siddhas[3]. The arrival of Muslims was a further blow to divisive structures though paradoxically cementing Brahmanism in small quarters. The contest of ideas assumed various shades of Bhakti and Sufism. The emergence and consolidation of the Sikh religion was embedded in this historical background of contestation between orthodoxies and rebellious ideas and practices.

It is very largely because of the Sikh religion that the literary activity of Punjabi Dalits has a long pedigree, the longest of all Indian vernaculars. The Sikh gurus had opened the doors of literacy for all Sikhs interested in the pursuit. Bhai Jaita (d. 1705), who was rechristened by Guru Gobind Singh as Jeevan Singh at the creation of Khalsa in 1699, happens to be the first Dalit poet from Punjab. He composed a long poem *Sri Gur Katha* which is an eyewitness account of important events surrounding Guru Gobind Singh's life. Sant Wazir Singh (1790-1859) attained the status of *Brahmgyani* and prolifically composed philosophical and cultural poetry, both in Punjabi and Braj bhasha. He attracted a number of people as his followers including five poet disciples coming from high castes. One of them, Nurang Devi, turns out to be the first woman Punjabi poet groomed under his tutorship. The next Dalit intellectual writer Giani Ditt Singh (1852-1901) emerged as a poet, teacher, polemicist, journalist, orator and ardent Sikh missionary who turned out to be the pillar of the Singh Sabha movement launched for the survival of Sikh religion that came under massive Brahmanical threat. He assumed editorship of the *Khalsa Akhbar*, a newspaper, in 1887 and continued it till his death in 1901. Meanwhile, he was also appointed a professor of Punjabi at the Oriental College, Lahore. He wrote more than fifty books on wide-ranging subjects, from love-lore to Sikh traditions, from history to ethics, from heroes to charlatans. Even being a leader in the limelight, he could not escape the overt and covert assault of untouchability from his fellow and follower Sikhs. Sadhu Daya Singh Arif (1894-1946) who came to master Gurmukhi, Urdu, Persian, Arabic and Sanskrit languages from informal teachers was the most popular intellectual poet of his time. His first poetical work *Fanah-dar-Makan* (Doomed House) was published when he had turned just 20. The work which made Daya Singh a household name through the length and breadth of the Punjab was *Zindagi*

Bilas (Celebration of Life) which was completed in 1916. It is in this work that his vast religious, spiritual and secular knowledge is manifest. Following the ancient assumption that average human life expectancy is 100 years, Daya Singh composed lyrical poems on each year. Overall, it is a touching didactic poetry that caught the masses' imagination, and became the most published, read or heard poetic creation next only to Waris Shah's *Heer*[4]. All four of them belong to what can be characterized as pre-Dalit consciousness era exhibiting a sound tradition of Punjabi Dalit literary creativity.

The age of Dalit consciousness begins with the appearance of Dr. B.R. Ambedkar (1891-1956) on the political and social map in the second half of 1920s. Incidentally, it beautifully brackets with the powerful Ad Dharam movement[5] of Dalits in Punjab that began in 1925. The movement produced a large number of poets and writers, though the most eminent happens to be Gurdas Ram Aalam (1912-1989), who becomes the first Punjabi poet with a heightened Dalit consciousness. Aalam had emerged as one of popular folk poets of the stage before the Partition. All the four books of his poems were full of social and economic issues of the oppressed-caste communities. On political and social issues, Aalam wrote like a revolutionary. No wonder, even the Naxalite young poet Pash[6] considered Aalam as the first revolutionary poet of Punjab. Hazara Singh Mushtaq (1917-1981) was different from his predecessor Dalit poets. He was an ardent nationalist, a flag-bearer of Indian National Congress and was also jailed a few times during the late-colonial rule for his nationalism. Of his seven books published, *Kissa Mazhbi Sikh Jodha* (Narrative of a Mazhbi Sikh Warrior)(1955) directly reflected his Dalit concerns. Though he does not chide 'Independence' in the context of the poor Dalits like Aalam, he expresses his disillusionment with the post-Independence developments. He brings in the socialist ideology to disparage the social and economic disparities, and calls the Dalits for a revolutionary rise in his book *Noori Ghazal* (Luminescent Ghazal) (1977).

The revolutionary rise that Punjab witnessed in the form of Naxalism in the late 1960s produced two Dalit poets with revolutionary as well as Dalit consciousness. They were Sant Ram Udasi (1939-1986) and Lal Singh Dil (1943-2007). Sant Ram Udasi was born in a Mazhabi Sikh[7] landless labour family. He grew up with a strong Dalit consciousness and had tried to see dignity in Sikh religion, but soon he experienced caste discrimination and untouchability present in the Sikh religion. During 1970s he emerged as one of the powerful radical poets and published three books of poetry. Lal Singh Dil was born in a Ramdasia Sikh (Chamar) family. He was training to be a basic school teacher when Naxalbari sucked him in. In the dream of a society free of caste and class, Dil saw a new dawn for the oppressed. He was arrested, incarcerated and tortured, more tortured because he was a Dalit, as his tormentors belonged to the dominant high castes. Dil was a sensitive poet and his poetry was true to life. The depiction of the experience of poverty, injustice and oppression was so real and told so well that he was hailed as the bard of the Naxalite movement in Punjab. It is remarkable that Dil's Dalit consciousness and identity was free from feelings of hatred, vengeance and malice. Though he remained and died a faqir, Dil has come to be acknowledged as one of the few best poets of last half century. The two powerful revolutionary Dalit poets were an upsurge on the Punjabi literary stage which had remained dominated by the upper-caste, upper-class litterateurs, and they became a major source for the bursting of Dalit literary energy in 1990s. If their poetry was looking for a revolutionary class change, it had the vivacity of Dalit identity which was capable of challenging the hegemonic discourses.

With the expansion of education there has been a progressive rise of Dalit writers in all genres of literature. It is against this rich backdrop of literary output of Dalits that a towering figure of Balbir Madhopuri as a great poet and writer can be adequately appreciated and understood. He has several influences on his personality from Guru Nanak, Marx, Ambedkar to Mangu Ram Mugowal and several other progressive personalities from social life and literature but he carved out his own ground to express his understanding with a critical gaze. These selected poems are a good enough mirror to see his inner self.

Rajkumar Hans
rajkhans@gmail.com

NOTES

1. **Mangu Ram Mugowal (1886-1980):** An Indian freedom fighter and leader of the lower castes in Punjab to fight against untouchability. He had migrated in 1909 to USA where he became a member of the Ghadar Party which was founded by Indians in USA to fight for India's independence. Upon his return to India in 1925, he became leader of the lower-caste people, organising them in opposition to the system of untouchability. He was instrumental in the foundation of the Ad Dharam Movement.
2. **Begumpura**: A verse by the Bhagti poet Ravidas who belonged to the caste of tanners. Here is a translation of this verse:

Begumpura, the City of No-Sorrows

They call it Begumpura
Pain and suffering have no place there
No worries about taxes or property
Neither fear, nor crime, nor greed, nor downfall
Now I have found an excellent home
Goodness reigns there always, my brother
That kingdom is eternal-immortal
There is no second or third, all are equal
It's populous and famous
The prosperous and contented live there
They roam about freely wherever they please
There are no prohibitions

Ravidas, the chamar now-set-free, says
They who reside here are my friends

3. **Nath Yogis and Siddhas:** a Shaivism-related group of monks which emerged around the 13th-century. They are sometimes called *Jogis* or simply *Yogis*, and are known for a variety of Siddha Yoga practices. Their tradition is known as Nath Sampradaya. They were primarily associated with the Yogic-traditions promoted by the great Nath saints, e.g. Matsyendranath, Gorakshanath.
4. **Waris Shah (1722-98):** was a great medieval Punjabi poet, author of the tragic love story Heer-Ranjha.
5. **Ad Dharam:** A religious sect founded by Mangu Ram Mugowal in 1920s for providing an identity for Dalits distinct from Sikhism and Hinduism, with Saint Ravidas as its spiritual Guru.
6. **Pash (1950-88):** Avatar Singh Sandhu, popularly known as Pash, the most dominant revolutionary poet emerging from the Naxalite movement in Punjab in 1970s; was gunned down by Sikh militants in 1988.
7. **Mazhbi Sikh:** Member of an untouchable caste who have left the Hinduism in favour of the Sikhism.

Biographical Note: Balbir Madhopuri

Balbir Madhopuri, poet, prose writer, translator and editor, was born in 1955 in Madhopur, a small village in district Jalandhar, Punjab in a Dalit family. At his birth he was named Balbir Chand. Later on, in 1990, he changed it to Balbir Madhopuri, dropping the latter part of his name 'Chand' because, he thought it connected him with a particular religion. His family consisted of ten members headed by his daadi (grandmother), and included his parents, he himself and six siblings. His father was an agricultural wage labourer who worked on the jat farmers' land. In addition, he was also a weaver and had his own loom at home for khadi and silk weaving. Madhopuri began school at the age of seven in his own village. After passing class V he joined another school in the village Gignowal about four and a half kms from Madhopur, a distance he travelled daily on foot, which he did barefoot until he got a pair of shoes when he came to class VIII. On his way to school he had to cross two small streams every day. He passed his High School from Gignowal in 1972 and then joined Government College at TandaUrmur, a small town in district Hoshiarpur. Here too he was a day scholar travelling daily to school partly by train and partly on foot. He passed his BA in 1977 and joined Lyallpur Khalsa College, Jalandhar for his MA course in Punjabi. He cleared his MA previous in 1978 but could not continue his studies as a regular student because he had to take up a job. He pursued his MA course privately and completed it in 1980.

Even while he was at school, he would help his father in agricultural and any other work on Sundays and during vacations. Although he and other boys of his caste were treated as untouchables by the local Gurudwara and were not allowed to go inside, the teachers at school did not discriminate. In fact, at school one of the brahmin teachers liked him very much and encouraged him to continue his studies because he was good at studies. He recalls how his clothes and his body remained infected with lice because he had only one set of clothing which could be washed only after a week or even ten days. At college, he had developed an interest in books, primarily those published from the Soviet Union. He also began to write poetry even at school, and when at college his poems and articles were published in newspapers. The poetry he wrote during this period was either romantic or revolutionary and he has not cared to retain it in any form. At college he had become a member of the CPI in 1974 and was secretary of its village branch. During the Moga Students' agitation in 1972, after a Naxalite student demonstration was fired at by the police, he was among the protestors who had signed a memorandum in their blood. About his religious beliefs he says there was no pressure of any kind from the family to believe in any God, his daadi herself had no faith in God. So, atheism came to him almost naturally for there was no temple in the village and the priests at the Gurudwara treated him and others like him so badly that it killed any reverence or faith in religion and God. But he remembers that on two occasions in his life he felt the need to invoke God. On one occasion, when he was in class VII and had to spend a few nights alone to guard the fields. The other was whenever he passed by a well on his way from his village to another. One of his uncles had committed suicide by jumping into this well.

While he was studying for his master's degree, he had joined the Food Corporation of India in 1978 and worked there till 1983. Here his workplace was in a village named Bhulath which was 21 kms from his village and he cycled to and fro. Something worse happened when he displeased his superior, who was a jat, by telling him to give up his sense of superiority. He was transferred to another workplace which was 35 km away. He would start for the place early morning when it was still dark and return home late after sunset doing 70 km each day on long dark and desolate roads. In 1983 he resigned from FCI and joined the Press Information Bureau (PIB), Ministry of Information and Broadcasting at its Jalandhar office and continued to work there till 1987. In March 1987 he joined at Delhi as assistant editor, Yojana (Punjabi), Publications Division, Ministry of I& B, Govt. of India and worked there till his retirement in 2015. He retired as Deputy Director, Publications Division.

For a fuller understanding of Madhopuri's life and struggles as a Dalit one has to go his autobiography, *Chhangiya Rukh* (The Lopped-off Tree, 2002), which is available in English translation as *Changiya Rukh: Against the Night–An Autobiography* published by Oxford University Press in 2010.

At present he is working as Director, Punjabi Sahit Sabha, New Delhi and editor of Samkali Sahit (quarterly), a publication of Sahit Sabha.

His Writings

At the beginning Balbir Madhpuri wrote romantic and revolutionary poetry, especially during his student days; all of which he has disowned.

He has so far published three volumes of poetry: *Maroothal da Birkh* (The Desert Tree, 1992), *Bhakhda Patal* (Smouldering Underworld, 1998) and *Meri Chonvi Kavita,* (My Selected Poetry, 2011). He came into prominence with the publication of his autobiography *Chhangiya Rukh* (*Swaijivani,* 2002) in Punjabi which has gone into 15 editions. It was translated into English by Tripti Jain and published as *Changiya Rukh: Against the Night–An Autobiography* by Oxford University Press in 2010. It was the first Punjabi Dalit autobiography to be translated into English. It has also been translated and published in some Indian languages including Hindi and Shahmukhi (in Pakistan in 2010). It has been serialized by 10 Punjabi, Hindi and Shahmukhi magazines and some of its chapters have been published in some English magazines and newspapers. *Changiya Rukh: Against the Night* by OUP was nominated for the Crossword Award in 2011. It was included in the 100 classics of the world for five years and is now considered a word class literature. It is now being translated into Russian by Moscow State University. It is likely to be published in 2021.

Madhopuri has also published *Sahitak Mulakatan* (Literary Conversations, 1995), *Samunder de Sung* (A travelogue, 1996), *Dilli Ik Virasat* (Delhi's Heritage, 1998) and *Ad Dharam De Bani* (Founder of Ad Dharam)*: Ghadri Baba Mangu Ram* (2010).

Apart from these writings Balbir Madhopuri has translated nearly 36 books into Punjabi from Hindi and English and other languages. He has also edited 40 books in Punjabi. His latest work 'Mitti Bol Pei', a work of fiction is in press.

Honours and Awards

His work has earned him many awards. Kav Purskar in (1994), Best Book Purskar (*Chhangiya Rukh*) in 2003 from Punjab Languages Department, Govt. of Punjab. Life-Time Achievement Award from Punjabi Academy, Delhi (2013); Translation Prize from Sahitya Akademi (2013) and Punjabi Academy, Delhi (2000). He was honoured by the former Prime Minister, Dr. Manmohan Singh, at the International Punjabi Conference, Delhi in 2018. In November 2019 he was honoured with the Principal Sant Singh Sekhon Award by Prof. Mohan Singh Memorial Foundation and Jagdev Singh Jasowal Charitable Trust. In February 2020 he was honoured by Government of Punjab and Guru Nanak Dev University for his contribution to Punjabi language, literature and culture.

Balbir Madhopuri lives in Delhi.

His e-mail address: madhopurihk@gmail.com

His Website: www.balbirmadhopuri.in

Translating Balbir Madhopuri

Balbir Madhopuri had already published two collections of his poetry in Punjabi before he came into prominence as a writer with his autobiography *Chhangiya Rukh* (The Lopped-off Tree) (Swaijivani) which was published in Punjabi in 2002 by Navyug Publishers, New Delhi and later in English translation in 2010 as *Changiya Rukh: Against the Night–An Autobiography* by Oxford University Press. His autobiography went into many editions and has been translated into other languages. It was the first Punjabi Dalit autobiography to be published in English. Madhopuri published his third collection of poetry *Meri Chonvi Kavita* (My Selected Poetry) in 2011.

The present anthology contains 34 poems, jointly selected by me and Madhopuri, and translated by me with help from him. It also contains the chapter *Being a Tenant*, extracted from his autobiography translated by Tripti Jain. The poems here have been selected from Madhopuri's third collection *Meri Chonvi Kavita* (2011) which in turn contains selections from his earlier two anthologies *Maruthal da Birkh* (The Desert Tree, 1992) and *Bhakhda Patal* (Smouldering Underworld, 1998). In addition, it contains a number of poems he wrote later but did not publish.

Dr. Raj Kumar Hans in his introduction to this collection has presented, in a very lucid manner, Balbir Madhopuri's view of the role of literature and poetry, which is the perspective of a Dalit poet as distinct from the mainstream critic's view of literature and poetry. He has further placed Balbir Madhopuri's poetry in the historical context of Dalit literature and poetry in Punjabi beginning with Bhai Jaita (1649-1704), a Mahzabi Sikh disciple of Guru Govind Singh (1666-1708), and its emergence as a powerful stream during and after the Naxalite movement in Punjab in the seventies of the last century.

It would have been perhaps better to let the poems speak for themselves because their directness and simplicity is by itself enough to communicate the intensity, the honesty and conviction with which Madhopuri writes. However, I would like to point out what, in my understanding, are the distinctive features of these poems. Apart from a presentation of Madhopuri's view of the nature and role of poetry as discussed by Dr. Raj Kumar Hans in his introduction, there is in these poems a strong autobiographical element. Madhopuri speaks of himself, his father, his mother, his wife and his daughter. He speaks of his father with pride even as he rues his naivety in giving away everything and getting nothing in return. He speaks of his mother as one who inspired him and made him aware of his father's achievements. He speaks with great affection of his wife who has, he says, stood by him in all his trials, and with apprehension for the safety of his daughter and fear that her dreams may come to nought. However, this autobiographical element has a deep underlying connection with his caste and community and the contemporary socio-political and economic environment in which he grew up and has struggled against and succeeded to a considerable extent. He is further able to connect his poetry with the broader world of his country and humanity at large. His dismay, not rage, is evident at what the Indian civilization has done to communities like his, and his deep concern that exclusion, discrimination and humiliations still continue both at the obvious and subtle psychological levels. Yet he does not become totally pessimistic and appeals to his fellow citizens on the other side to bring about a change and end this centuries-old curse. A few poems also talk about the dark days of militancy in Punjab when 'a clayey figure/turns into a tiger on wielding a gun', and a few are meditative in tone and tenor.

Madhopuri's poetry has a distinctive flavour provided by his use of imagery and symbolism ranging from Punjab's shared history and traditions, the Indian classical tradition, to the colloquialisms of the rural Doaba region of Punjab and the imagery from the modern urban landscape. Alas, a translation can retrieve only some of these images but perhaps still convey the painful intensity of the poet's experience and the urgency of his message. That is my hope.

I have added, with the permission of OUP and consent of Balbir Madhopuri, a chapter from Tripti Jain's translation of Madhopuri's autobiography as a kind of finale to the poems I have translated. This chapter *Being a Tenant* clearly demonstrates that although Madhopuri has personally overcome the economic disability to which his community has been subjected he has not succeeded in overcoming the social ostracization practised by the dominant castes. One must add that he is so persistently reminded of his caste, wherever he is, that it seems to be engulfing his life and his poetry like a nuclear mushroom cloud.

Working with Madhopuri on his poems during these translations has been a very pleasant and rewarding experience and has been a constant reminder that the upper caste (to which I belong) communities have a long way to go to shed and overcome their deep-seated aversions, prejudices, and totally false sense of superiority, and atone for the centuries old-crime our civilization has continued to commit.

Delhi **T.C. Ghai**

Poems

In Search of Poetry

These days I go
in search of poetry
as someone in the desert should go
in search of a tree.

In our times
poetry has become so insensitive
in truth, lost its way
become empty of social concerns
has forgotten
its proud tradition
of fighting against the throne:
the feeling for the suffering
swings from the hangman's noose.

In these times, my contemporaries,
poetry has learnt
like a river
to flow within its banks,
like a bullock-cart
to move on the beaten track.

If the mainstream is a dark tunnel
what can live words do?
Meanings can only wear out.

What a turn!
Mother, in your poetry's sheath
meaning has become
a rust-eaten kirpan.
Words are infected with lecherous worms
like computer virus.
Even then I keep searching
for a weak-bodied, dark-skinned
insignificant man a poem
a civilization like Mohenjo-Daro.

My beloved poetry,
don't go away from the earth
like a spaceship;
don't reserve your words
only for love tales;
come back again
like the newly sprouted shoots
on leafless trees,
like dew drops on grass.

These days I go
in search of poetry
as someone in the desert should go
in search of a tree.

Poetry is Not Mere Words

Poetry is not mere words.
It is
the flight of a man
without wings.

Poetry is not mere words.
It's the agonizing cry
of a black partridge
snapped up by an eagle
as it flies out of a sugarcane field.
It's the frenzied outcry
of a deer terrified in the wild.
It's the story of leaves precariously dangling
from the branch of a tree.

Poetry is not mere words.
It is
the meanings emanating from words
that have lost their character
in the polluted environment;
even then they are

like monsoon showers in the peak of summer,
like stars on a moonless night.

Poetry is not mere words.
It is
the pain of the failure
to conquer the Red Fort of life.
It is the inexpressible story
of the seething waters of a river
that rose and fell.

Poetry is not mere words.
It is
the dance of limpid waters
and waves
struggling against banks
for equality;
roads marching towards a destination.

Poetry of my times,
your words are deadly silent.
This is debasement of their meaning.
Poetry, don't be a slogan
become a voice;
not burning coal
but cosy wings of a hen
over its shivering-in-cold chicks.

Poetry is not mere words.
It is
the flight of a man
without wings.

Poetry, Tell Them

Poetry,
tell them who pluck flowers:
Fragrances can't be shut up.
And tell them
that for cactus to bloom
in the burning sand of the desert
to keep smiling in every season
is its very nature.

Poetry,
speak to Sahiban[1]:
She should not, like the spider, weave
with the strands of her fancies
a golden web around herself
that Mirza[2] will return one day
bringing down the moon
and stars plucked from the skies.

And tell her
he is busy in search of a livelihood,
waiting for electricity beside his tube-well;

and no one knows when
Farhad's[1] Sutlej-Jamna[2] link canal would flow
and the peasant's budding crop begin to bloom.

Poetry,
tell the fish confined in a bottle
that oceans are infested with crocodiles;
and the colourful fishes
have returned
from across the seven seas
having licked the stones of self-indulgence.

Poetry,
tell the white pigeons
not to behave like parrots;
but when the sky is a cage
to fly away in a flock
against the winds.

Poetry,
tell those insects
it's better
to fly on rainy-season wings
and be burnt on flames
than to crawl and
be squelched under heels.

Poetry,
tell the tired bull
he should shift the earth
onto the other horn.

A Wish for My Poetry

I don't want
my poems
to fall into a river
like monsoon nullahs
and lose their selfhood.

I don't want
my poems
to join the poetry-stream
whose scriptures
fragment a vast field
into enclaves;
reserve the velvety green grass
for those on top of the pyramid
and forbid dark-skinned people like me
to open their third eye.

I want
my poems
to be dedicated to the birds
who in search of their feed

transgress the village bounds
and alight in this or that courtyard
unbothered by the high and low
rooftops of households.

I just want
my poems
to join the stream of poetry
that narrates
the tales of Eklavya[1] and Banda Bahadur[2]
the struggles of Pir Buddhu Shah[3],
and Pablo Neruda's[4] compassion.

I don't want
My poems
to fall into a river
like monsoon nullahs
and lose their selfhood.

My Caste

My caste is always with me
like my complexion
like my shadow.
We are so rolled into one
I'm nothing
except my caste,
in the city in the village
here or across the seas.

I try very hard to hide, to cloak
wear a hundred masks
but it shows itself
again and again
like the white hair
after the dye has worn off,
like the bodies peeping
through tattered clothes.

I wish to be rid of it
like someone wanting a divorce
but they tell me

impress upon me
this bond stays on birth after birth...
nothing to think about.

Finally
the bow is strung
with arrows of reason,
that pierce both present and past.
Blood boils within
like an earthquake
and then
the gaps seem to be bridging
east-west, right-left.

My caste is always with me
like my complexion
like my shadow.
We are so rolled into one
I'm nothing
except my caste,
in the city in the village
here or across the seas.

Tsunami Waves

The tsunami waves
swept away many things:
briny rocky shores
living things
sea creatures
trees and humans
beautiful natural landscape.

The waves overwhelmed
even God's own houses,
of this religion and that religion,
where people passed by awestricken
trembling with fear.

And in no time land became water;
in the blink of an eye
present became past.
People recalled:
'Death is a great leveller.'
Yet the survivors reversed the tune.
The living labelled the dead:

One high, the other low
one touchable, the other untouchable.

In this way on the seashore
the *not-humans* were left hungry-thirsty,
bereft of help and hope
in the demonic laughter of the *humans*.
And the tsunami waves
that had demolished the rocky shores
one and all
could not knock down
the towering walls of hatred
rising in the human hearts.

In the aftermath
on the now calm sea's wide shore,
let someone reflect
and say:
Let us push our boat
into the sea of humaneness
like the waves embrace each other
merge into each other
catch the poisonous fish.
Come let us play this game.

Sanskriti

Now
even the deserts
have become green
Crops are blooming
even in the barren lands
The natural landscape too
has changed
Yet the Varna system[1]
built into my Sanskriti
stays as it was even now

Now
even the unbounded space
has shrunk
Like the colours of the sunlight
the seven continents too
have become one
The Berlin wall too
has crashed like glass
collapsed into a heap of dust

Yet the stony doors of my Sanskriti
no key can unlock
no argument batter down

Now even
the ice-loaded mountains
are melting
Waters in the oceans
are warming up
And at places hot and strong winds
have started blowing
And my Sanskriti
like the consumer culture
still sticks different labels
on human beings

A Man Lighter than Straw

Many a time
I'm dwarfed
like a beheaded tree
that supports
overhead power lines;
feel lopped-off out of season
when casually
someone wants to know my religion.

Many a time
this clayey body becomes thinner
than water;
words
fall off the tongue
like leaves from a tree
in autumn; and
I feel I am drowning
and the earth doesn't open up to swallow me
when suddenly
someone wants to know
my caste.

Many a time
my heart's sky
is overcast
with clouds of deep sadness
when
in the metropolitan air
the bird
flying freely
full of bird chatter
in search of a feed
sits down folding his wings
when out of the blue someone
wants to know his native state
first the village, then the mohalla.

Many a time
in fact, quite often
the bird in flight
is shot down with arrows
now of religion, now of caste
now of mohalla, now of Varna.

He Said

He said
For long I have followed in your footsteps
now you follow in mine
They said
We have the head
and you have the feet
The duty of the feet is to walk

He said
For long I have been your yes-man
now listen to me
They said
We have the tongue
and you the ears
Their duty is to listen

He said
I was made homeless by you
now give me back my home
They said
The Adivasi's home is the jungle

We shall spread the jungle air
It's a sin to go against the wind

He said
I am a blinkered ox
allow my weary limbs to rest
unblinker my eyes
They said
Your duty is not to see
but to shut your eyes after seeing

He said
I shall move against the wind
They said
It's now impossible
to stop the wind

Song of the Land

The land has begun to sing
O Patwari
Write a piece in our name

Don't wield the soil planer unevenly
O Patwari
Awakened fields want justice

Stop these dubious measurements
O Patwari
Sons of the soil have only one village

Parrots nibble at milky corn
O Patwari
We can't tolerate this sin

Having lopped off the branches
O Patwari
Don't hope for a cool shade

The cropped hay puts out shoots again
O Patwari
Give us our share of three-arm length of space

The earthly gods will drown
O Patwari
They will be made to fly without wings

Against the Wind

They went to mow the grass
and came back as mothers
O father
the cow-like
virgins

Harvest-like daughters
in your courtyard
O father
Hordes of Rahu-Ketus[1]
line up

They who sow don't reap
O father
Save your turban
even if you starve

Flames rise
in Eklavya's heart
O father
The brave boy's arrows
are pills of death

Villages have become Belchi and Pipran[1]
O father
Eagles besiege
the girl-sparrows

Fish swim
against the current
O father
Flocks fly today
against the wind

Mother Tells

Mother
turns towards me
and tells:
Before you were born
he took on the mountains
broke their pride
straightened up pathways
bridged the gorges
glared at the high mountains.

Mother
shines like a sparkler
and tells me:
At the time of your birth
he like Farhad
dug canals night and day
in the Shivalak Hills
that waters should flow
that deserts should bloom
and the barren land become fertile.

Mother
tells me
as she laughs:
When you began to toddle,
stumbled as you learnt to run
he became a bridge over rivers
stretching his shrunken waist and rock-like chest
so distances be shortened
and caravans could go across.

Mother
tells me
though baulked by something
she still goes on:
He shouted at the top of his voice:
I ploughed the fields
I built the palaces
I saved the country from sinking.
And they
quietly proclaimed:
You deserve only to be whipped.
Age after age
you are born only to serve.

Mother
tells me,
as if saddling up a horse,
tells me again and again
of the few struggling, rebellious people
among countless men and women;
and I only see
my old father's
drooping, wrinkled face;

in his eyes
deep redness like burning coal.
And now
reflecting mother's words
again and again
I rush towards the horse.

My Old Man

My old man
still believes
lines drawn on water
are lines etched on stone.

Watering other's flowering plants
he himself blooms into a flower;
gently patting the backs of milch cattle
he prays for the family's well-being.
As he holds the plough's handle
he wishes for the welfare of all;
becomes mud with mud.

With his hands he has brought
the green, the white and the blue revolutions;
but through his body
still flows a dry river.

Out there, in the peak of summer, scorched weak bodies
and inside
shining smooth shapes,

hearts seeking bodily pleasures;
and his inherited-ancestral belief
tells him again and again
this is just the play of destiny.

Now and then, he wonders,
even though crocodiles infest the seas
yet so many fish swim there freely.
There's the sky for birds to fly
and places to build nests.
And what do I have?
This land of a *glorious* Sanskriti!
My own progeny
to perpetuate the tradition of slavery!

Occasionally, he reflects
and searches
for meaning in the words:
'There's delay, but not darkness',
and looks at his horny palms
for the vanished or vanishing lines.

My old man
still believes
lines drawn on water
are lines etched on stone.

The Horse and My Old Man

For centuries
have ridden on his back
the inhuman Varna system
religions of this land
satanic misdeeds

When his bare body
is whipped
he doesn't walk
he gallops
forgetting
the cotton plugs in his ears
blinkers on his eyes
the bit in his mouth
summer or winter

They at whose doors
he stands bound
by Smritis
by Codes
tell us

in a light mood
tauntingly:
He sleeps on the sly
never seen him sitting
only seen him laid flat
when shoes are hammered into his soles

Fed on husk
straw and leftovers
he is so agile
he defeats time
so powerful
even lightning is shamed

But these days
he has become mulish
begun to rear up on his hind legs;
and now to me
it seems
that blue horse
is my own old man
a new tune
of a wearied human heart

For centuries
have ridden on his back
the inhuman Varna system
religions of this land
satanic misdeeds

Before I Fall into the River of Sleep

My wife lying beside me
never knows
when I, lying in the room,
on a clear night
start chasing
a small cloud
riding in the lap of the wind;
push a boat
to reach the light shining
across the swollen river;
start ransacking my books
for the butterfly wings
tucked in a book in my childhood.

She does not even know
when, galloping down the road
I break through the red signal
and collide against a dolphin;
when I sweat from every pore,
as if Iraq were reminded of America;

as if I were reminded of Punjab
while travelling in a bus;
and then as if
of the garbled couplets of a perfect ghazal.

My wife lying beside me
never knows
when, piercing the darkness
through closed windows and doors,
I drop down
with heavy wings
as if I were in debt
But in truth
in a ramshackle house
I wait
for the sun to rise
to see a smile
on my little girl's face.

Consolation

Don't fear the water's rising wave.
It will by itself
turn into an eddy;
waters after all must flow
under the bridges,
my dear wife.

Don't ever wake my daughter
lying asleep in her cradle,
who, watching the stars coming out of a sparkler,
herself turns into a sparkler;
and let her dream
of filling her lap
by plucking the stars
swimming in the sky.
And don't ever tell her
that her father's dreams
of holding the rainbow,
of bringing down the moon
and placing it as a medallion on his wife's forehead
have come to naught.

Don't tell
my butterfly-like
butterfly-catching
lighter-than-flowers,
frightened-like-a-hare little daughter
that the procession of sins is endless;
or else her dolls would drop down her hands.
Rather you should tell her
that her father holds
a pigeon in his left
and an eagle in his right hand.

You should let my fragrance-like daughter
draw pigeons and doves
in her notebook as before,
and set them to fly.
My good wife
don't be afraid of the whirlwinds
for they are godless.

Don't fear the tidal waves,
my dear wife,
waters after all must flow
under the bridges.

The Sunshine's Journey

The break of day
is like a siren for her
As soon as she wakes
she begins to water the plants
and the flowers big and small
bloom and spread their fragrance

And I
slurping my tea
turn the pages of the newspaper
dig into the political news–
how one faction
has floored the other
and I am reminded
of particular slokas of Tulsi[1] and Manu[2]

That's how
her morning turns into noon
and she spreads the shade of her being
on the blooming flowers

and the difference
between the tall mulberry tree
and my sunshine
seems to disappear

That's how her noon
mellows
That's how her noon
has mellowed

Whenever I return riding my mare
through dark and narrow lanes
she, standing at the door,
catches the mare's rein
and the tidal waves inside her
recede in no time
A light shines in her eyes
and the earth seems
peaceful as before

That's how
her morning begins
That's how
her noon descends
That's how
her noon mellows
That's how
her high noon has mellowed

My Life

(to my wife)

Ever since she has joined me
we are one-and-one eleven.
My feet sail above the ground
and I have left far behind
the jungle of deep sorrows,
piles of hatred.
I have laid down before her love
weapons of anger-resentments,
of animosities.

She has sowed
in my heart
the seeds of a new revolt
just as she is nurturing
in her body
our heir to come.

She has covered
the labyrinth of my vices-imperfections

just as the skin hides
the network of blood vessels and entrails.
But she freely bares
the journey of my feet
that have negotiated ditches-bumps
left-right, back-front;
how I swam across swollen rivers;
my forthright utterances
in public.

She is very secretive
like thoughts dissolved in blood.
Sometimes
why, many times,
she calls me Krishna
and herself Radha,
me Shiva
and herself Parvati;
seems building bridges
between Aryans-n-non-Aryans
and for my sake
she has absorbed much
inside her
just as the earth the poisonous chemicals.
When we go out
to rent a house
or face insults
at religious places
she with her questioning eyes
digs into the conscience of humans.
Then she shines even more
like the sun
and filled with joy she says,

our heir, born of our seed,
will bring heaven on earth
spread his eyelids for people to walk on.

I stare at her
goggle-eyed and
see the present and future
through the past.

An Oasis

(to my friend Purshottum Sharma)

At times
he is distant like the sun
and close like the sunshine
At times
musing on my adolescence days
I am filled with warmth
On occasions
his speech scorches

Whenever I unroll
the folds of the past
he becomes
sometimes my crutches
sometimes my wings

Whenever I descend
into dark endless caves
or boggy hells
he is visible as the steadfast polestar

Sometimes he is brilliant sunshine
Sometimes an umbrella
Sometimes a protective sword
Sometimes the Lakshman Rekha

During a drought
he becomes a dew drop
In the desert
he becomes an oasis

When the Hot Wind Blows

Now when
the hot wind blows
Ichharan's[1] gardens are devastated;
many faces disappear,
night's silence reigns
even during the day;
then reminding myself
of the turmeric-pale faces
of my cotton-soft daughter
and sunshine-like wife
I rush back home.

Now when
someone writes on the wind
draws a line on water
then
swans drown themselves
in the limpid waters of lakes;
and I
like cowards
become a creeper around

my soft-as-kitten daughter,
who is just beginning to babble,
and my mulberry-shoot like wife;
and like someone sick
I enclose my small world
within my eyes.

Now when
an earthquake shakes the mountains
perched above the piece of earth that's my share,
lust descends like rain,
tidal waves rise unstoppable
in the sea of sensuality;
then
the toy-like daughter of mine
erects mud walls
between me and my share of the world.
And I
think of raising the height
of walls that enclose my home,
for who knows when the blind wind
would come crashing through the threshold.

Waiting for a Cool Breeze

The sunshine is dead at high noon
no shade either
Trees are bereft of branches
only few remain
Anthills have risen under every tree
No shade to sit under
The five rivers dyed in red
shed tears where they are

Pistols and guns grow
where flowers and ears of corn grew
These demand blood for watering
One is at a loss
Why no one stops the hailstorms
is a deep mystery
They reap what they sow
yet they complain

The skies swing in deep hopelessness
stars fall
courtyards are drowned in mourning

walls shiver
How can one stop this wind
spreading all around
Bodies tough as stone wear down
in the brackish streams from the eyes

Cypress-like bodies should not fall
A crane should not stray from its flock
Doves should coo in courtyards
A cool breeze should blow from across
People should not come to mourn in droves
Nor Bakki[1] be without its rider
Winds should become fragrant
Minds glow with light

Sky is Witness

Many eyes
remained unrolled on deserted pathways
to lovingly welcome someone
But the pathways had devoured
the footprints of the home-comers

Many fields
waited for the touch of the soft feet
that never weighed heavy on them
like those of strangers

Many oxen
bellowed for the hands
whose one pat
would relieve their daylong fatigue

Dogs like Moti
like members of the family
sat disheartened
wondering for whom
to wag their tails

A heart would suddenly
start beating fast
on seeing a clayey figure
turn into a tiger on wielding a gun

The sky has absorbed
the tragedy of the five rivers
the stabs of the conspiring winds
the tearfulness of exploding clouds
the memory of falling stars
the sound of tender shoots cracking

Bring Back the Seasons

Bring back the seasons
in which
the grass trampled under feet
can feel alive
and grows tall during the night
by four-fingers breadth
bitter cucumbers remain no longer bitter
sugarcane stalks become sweet
and soap nuts too become sweet

Bring back the seasons
in which
the breeze from the east blows
and brings
dark thick clouds
the monsoon rains pour down
earth's surface cools
and the seven-coloured swing
spans the sky

Bring back the seasons
in which
the noon sunshine laughs
the mango trees blossom
heart's peacock begins to dance
eyes are strung up with love
colourful sparklers are held in hands
and the youth
walk with a spring in their strides

Bring back the seasons
bring back the sons
watching whom
Ichhran's[1] eyes
light up
and Salwan's[2] withered garden
becomes green again

They Don't Want

They don't want
the sandalwood saplings
to grow into trees
and radiate fragrances
in all directions
into the polluted air
during unhappy times
They want
to divide the waters
to divide the saints
They want bloody streets
where Shakunis[1] and Narads[2] roam
to light a four-wicked lamp
on the grave of shared hearth and home

They don't want
trees to become woodland,
to grow bigger, thicker and blossom
They want
the forest trees
to stand apart

or they want bamboos to rub against one another
and become the fire god
The powerful have so many black spells
in their repertory

They don't want
they don't tolerate
coloured umbrellas over others' heads
any warmth in the dead cold seasons
peals of laughter spilling in the behadas[1]
They want
the rising waters
to recede
like the boil in milk
to nip the thought about to fertilize
They keep devouring the shades of trees
at noontide
the addresses
of the sons of this land

They don't want
to melt tridents and swords
into ploughshares
to plough new fields
They want
to sharpen their edges
by hammering them again and again
They want to plant peepul trees
on their chests
like those growing or grown
across the borders.

Life - I

Life
the globe-like ball
stitched by rolling together shreds of cloth
discarded by the tailor–
the illusory symbol of 'unity in diversity'
when unstitched breaks up
into a continent, a subcontinent, an island.

Life
a scrap dealer's godown
where there is
a clutter of damaged soft, colourful polythene bags
to be changed into flowers
and the iron scrap
for 'sardar'[1], the desert hero's chest.

Life
the rooster
with a fine crest
that becomes the sacrificial feast
for Dhantrans[2] of politics
after it has crowed for votes.

Life
inside one's body and soul
is father, husband and brother
or a long smouldering cigarette
that becomes ash
without burning.

Sometimes
life becomes a rebellious wind
sometimes a horse galloping
with the bit in his mouth
to reach a destination;
and life wonders
and often wishes
the bull carrying the earth
should shift it on to the other horn.

Life - II

Life
I wish to live with you
like a plant with mud
greenness with the leaf
the landscape with eyes

Life
I wish to be bonded
with you
like the fish with the sea
warmth with the sun
fragrance with flowers

Life
I wish to negotiate
the ups and downs
like a boat on the waves
like a mountain herdsman
going up and down the hills

Life
every day I wish
to become a cloud
over burning desert
or cosy wings over chicks
shivering-dying with cold

Life
I wish to expand
like one face of all the seven seas
like sunshine of all the seven colours
and one green tree

Life
I wish to live with you
like a plant with mud
greenness with the leaf
the landscape with eyes

Sunshine and Shade Walk Together

Water flowed away under the old bridge;
the river-swell receded.

The duck's body remains dry,
though waters shake and splash.

Although the frame is old
the mirror reflects new light.

Lest it should touch the sky
the wind chases away the cloud.

The wind gently brushed past;
the tree became dumbfounded.

Why do you blink your eyes?
Sunshine and shade walk together.

The branch bends low with the weight of the fruit;
the tree sways with the wind.

When the East wind blows
the tree blossoms faster.

The Contracting Circle

Many things have been left behind,
like my childhood:
my village, my people
fields dearer than sons
trees like Mirza'a Jhand[1]
witnesses to love tales.

Like waters that have flowed past,
this clayey figure
has crossed many landmarks:
breath after breath
years two and a half times
the number of chapters in the Gita;
walls of love and infatuation
and mountain peaks.

Have forgotten many things,
like dreams:
the flight of birds
my ancestry

my language
and the land of Siyals'[1] progeny.

There's much I have with me
like my wife and children:
a few names and places
rivalries over love
relationships that have evaporated
horrifying scenes of fights
over water sharing
and this wing-clipped bird thinks only,
like blood coursing through the body,
of picking the feed that lies scattered.

Waves

That moment is terrifying
when one is fighting a Mahabharat with oneself:
one hears neither the sound of weapons
nor sees the flames issuing from agnivaans;
at times one is crushed under time's chariot wheels
at others one is run over by the wheels of artha and kama.

Worse than this is the time
when from the gulmohar swaying in your courtyard
green leaves begin to fall
and petals from the deep red flowers;
when the tree becomes leafless in spring
and is unable to express its helplessness.

Many a time in no time
the scene changes
and one sees
ever flowing rivers,
watches flowers blooming in all seasons
and forgets the troublesome
active service in Basra,

and like a victorious soldier
returns home for the love of land
to water the flowers
in one's courtyard.

During Moments of Silence

Many a time a man sitting alone in a room
is not alone
At times watching a butterfly fluttering its wings
he starts counting down
the years of his life
like the countdown of a satellite launch
Sometimes in the company of a butterfly
he soars into the sky in short spurts

Sometimes groping in dark tunnels
looking for a lighted window
he is Abhimanyu
Sometimes he is fighting a Mahabharat
with himself
Sometimes he is
pierced with arrows of broken relationships
and yet he sends the doves flying
Sometimes like Amur[1] overstepping boundaries
he flows like a river of friendship
and sometimes he becomes a pucca bridge

Sometimes on a full moon night
he becomes an island surrounded by water
Sometimes his selfhood shines through
Sometimes he meditates on togetherness

Waves in the Mind

Crossing the jungle of roads
passing through life's blind alleys
I see staring at me
milky corncobs as if spinning cotton
budding wheat and paddy
stalks more fragile than glass;
and others, sown beside them, withering.
I am witness to this silent lamentation.

Fissures in drought-stricken fields
raise into consciousness
the cracks in the elder's heels;
oxen biting into withered stubble
like sisters, born one after the other,
clawing at their mother's dry teats;
and father's silent prayers
for flowers to bloom for everyone
for the drying crops to green again;
and his words said and unsaid
I quietly translate to myself.

The water-channel dug on the southern side
seems becoming wider and wider,
which neither I nor my upper-caste friend
could ever go across
rebelling against the banks.
The river of friendship wants to flow,
unmindful of mud or marble,
because water seeks its own level.

Red Speech

(After the break-up of the Soviet Union)

The sun set in the East
the West broke out into dance

The West wind so blew
the red flower withered

The crane flies the whole night
to see the sunrise

Small and big clouds join hands
to come down as rain

Greenness of trees deepens
when the East wind blows

Dark clouds from the East come down
the trees rejuvenate

Clouds float loaded with water
to come down on dry land

The flood waters can't be dammed
howsoever hard they try

One day it will explode like a volcano
the fire that smoulders underneath the straw

A Letter

My friend residing in the capital,
I don't know why
now Delhi to us and
your village to you seem far away.

To me it seems you would know
where, in the village,
we used to hear the recitation:
'We are all a brotherhood
the progeny of One
people of the same Creation',
we now hear the talk
of your God and my God.

Just a churn in water.

My friend
you know it well
lines can't be drawn on water,
dreams can't be unravelled.
The fields where

we grazed our cattle
played hide-and-seek
many now
wish to draw lines there
and harbour the illusion to shut up fragrances.
Who doesn't know
the breeze filled with fragrances
can't be stopped even by Koh-e-Qaf.[1]

Friend,
we, the boatmen,
wish to carry people across the river
but here now the mischief-makers
want to drown
mid-stream
daughters of the Siyals
brave sons of Takhat Hazara[2];
or they wish to divert
the flow of rivers
so we can't see
the deep red of the rising day.

Friend,
come, let's
infuse perfumes in the air
light lamps in the darkness
and sing:
'We are all a brotherhood
people of the same Creation'.
Then neither Delhi to us
nor our village to you
would seem far away
and our trees would blossom.

Come, My Contemporary

Come, my contemporary,
let's meet again
just as two pathways meet,
merge into each other
like a river in the sea.

Come, my contemporary,
let's sing, in the marketplace,
the death song
of the *Sanatani* Sanskriti
that has divided mankind again and again
that is devoid of reason.

Come, my contemporary,
let's bury deep the *living* words
whose meanings stink,
that don't still forget *the dead mother*
and lacerate so many hearts every day.

Come, my contemporary,
let's give up the Kissa[1] tradition

give up the Sanskriti of Sanskrit.
Let's load with stones the boat
in which our life is living death.

Come, my contemporary,
let's fight another Mahabharat
write a different sixteenth chapter
dam the river of fire
and send the white pigeons
across the dividing lines.

Come, my contemporary,
let's bring under the shade of the word
the life that is a desert
plant flowers in barren lives
and fulfill the duty of words.

Come, my contemporary,
let's find words
that mean sunshine, air, the sea,
that are passionate like a warrior
that spread fragrance into the sky.

Come, my contemporary,
let's meet again
just as two pathways meet,
merge into each other
like a river in the sea.

❑❑❑

Being a Tenant

(An extract from *Changiya Rukh: Against the Night*)

A baraat (groom's party) of eleven reached the village of my in-laws, on the occasion of my wedding. The women of the bride's family sang welcome songs, and they also began singing sithnis–abusive ditties, usually sung by the women of the bride's family. These are some of verses they sang:

You can take the money
from our village,
and get a band to come
with the groom.
The baraat doesn't look good,
you shameless ones,
You should be ashamed of
yourselves.
Or
The baraatis could not get a band
They came beating their bellies.

These women were making loud comments about us, 'They say that the groom is an officer–but they haven't even got a photographer to make a video film ... as if they have come only to take the bride...some show of grandeur and gaiety is necessary ...'

'They say that they don't want any dowry!' This was another voice.

'Who notices or cares if they get something for free!' This came from another voice. 'If not now, they will ask for it later on–it is only said for form's sake, sister. Later, they want more.'

After the wedding ceremony of two and half hours, the worry which had been eating me for the last few months again reared its head. This was the worry of our bridal night and our married life. I was full of fears of all sorts. I was under a great deal of pressure, and felt as if a mountain had fallen on me. I had lost about ten kilos of weight in the last few months. Some of my friends had even teased me about it, 'You are losing weight even before you are married, but don't worry, you will put on a lot of weight after your marriage. It works on one like desi ghee.'

On the fifth day after our wedding, we were in Delhi. Within a month and half, I had regained my lost weight and felt happy and content. But this happiness was short-lived, and within four or five months, harsh realities had clipped the wings of my elation.

The wedding expenses of two younger sisters and my elder brother, and the house, had all created a big financial mess for me, and I was trying my best to extricate myself from it. I had been taking loans from my provident fund at frequent intervals, and my take-home salary was now less than two thousand. Out of this meagre sum, I kept a third for myself and a third I sent home to Madhopur. The rest, I gave my elder brother, for I was living with him.

Within six years we had three children. My third sister had also been married off. The loan instalments being deducted from my salary had increased. The rising cost of living and escalating expenses had added to my problems, and also to the mental tension. Then, one day, my elder brother told me rather sharply, 'Every month you say that you will move into some other accommodation, but you don't go. The eight hundred you give me–do you think that it is enough for running the household? Your friends always visit us in hordes. When you live on your own, only then will you really know how expensive everything is, and how to run a household.'

'What about the eight hundred I send home? Is that not worth anything?' I retorted. 'You keep telling me to borrow from my provident fund and that we will somehow manage.'

'You move out, we also want to live happily and on our own,' My bhabhi, clinched the argument.

To me it seemed that all my plans to help take the family forward had been demolished, the way Babri Masjid had been a few days back. There was no basis on which a compromise could be worked out. Perhaps they had not given much thought to the future of the family. Perhaps I was nothing more than a money-making machine for them!

That very morning I took a friend, who happened to be my wife's cousin, Misrdeep Bhatia, on a house-hunting trip, and succeeded in renting a room in Munirka, after a long search and various difficulties.

My office and my eldest daughter's school were only a kilometer from there. The house was new and we cooked and ate our first meal in new utensils. Our five-member family slept on one bed under one quilt. Neither did we have another bed nor was there any bed linen. I did, however, have plenty of books.

Madan, who was like a younger brother, came to see us with his wife and twin children after a couple of days. My wife and I looked askance at one another.

'Madan, let's finish this stuff first, it is not very good.' I said putting some biscuits and sugar before them. My salary had already been used to buy some essentials for the kitchen.

'This was her first visit with her babies! We didn't have even ten rupees to give them,' my wife said, almost in tears.

I was preoccupied with my own thoughts. When I returned from work, the house owner, seated in front of the house, pulling on his hookah, would often ask, 'Bhai, don't be annoyed, but which caste do you belong to?'

'We are Sikhs,' I would answer, adjusting my turban.

'Don't be angry, once I was travelling by train from Agra to Delhi and a sardar and his wife were also travelling with me. They were well-dressed and the man appeared to be educated. I asked him about Punjab, and learnt many things...'

'Really?'

'... And I asked him about his caste. Like you, he also said, that he was a Sikh. I told him, "Sikhs also have caste, Which caste do you belong to?" He hesitated at first, and then he said that he was a Ramdasia.'

'Good, your time was well spent.'

'When he told me that he was a Ramdasia, what more could I talk to him about–I turned my face the other side,' the elderly Gujjar proudly told me.

'If he had lied to you and told you that he belonged to a higher caste?'

'... Then, he would have sinned,' and with this he picked up a bottle of rum lying near him, poured some into a glass and drank it, neat!

I disliked this old man. I felt as if a new phase of humiliation had begun. Wearied of this daily interrogation, my hunt for a new house began all over again.

I went to Sector VII in R.K. Puram to a family we knew well. It was winter and the landlady was seated on the roof, knitting.

'Give me an advance of five thousand–we will give these quarters to you; these days, these class IV quarters are going for Rs 10,000. We, of course, know each other.'

We settled happily in the new house. But my daughter's school, which was in Sector III was very far away. I didn't own a cycle and there was no other mode of transport except the local bus. I had to fetch her from school in the blistering heat of the summer afternoon and drop her home, and then rush off to office. I would often think what a difference would it have made if my elder brother had let us live with him till the end of the school session? The skies would not have fallen! Time and again, I would recollect what my mother had said, 'Now, there are three houses. If only they had lived together till the marriage of the two younger children, and set up separate households after that!'

We had lived in that house for five months, when one day, a stout woman walked in, adjusting her sari, and started shouting, 'Who are you? How did you come into my quarters without my permission?'

Fresh trouble in the form of this woman added to our woes. She sat down on the bed and began talking to us in a very arrogant tone. We looked at each other. The children whispered to us, 'When will this "Tuntun" leave... she is sitting on our bed! Where will we sleep?'

'Had I been receiving rent then I would have had no objection,' she said, after she had taken some tea.

'They took five thousand advance from us, and were taking Rs 500 a month as rent. They had told us that everything had been regularized. You can live here and needn't worry. Five hundred would be deducted from the advance,' we told her about the arrangements we had made.

'That means a thousand in rent! She herself was only giving five hundred as rent!' she retorted. We were astonished at what we had heard. She gave us some time and, somehow, we managed to pay her the back rent.

Actually, the family we had known was aware of the orders of the Supreme Court and that there was going to be an investigation about the subletting of these government quarters. They had taken advantage of the opportunity, and giving us the key, had made their escape. When we asked them about the fraud that they had perpetrated on us, we were thoroughly scolded, 'Any agent charges three months' rent as commission, and you go on complaining! You are insulting us by repeatedly asking about the money–don't you dare do it again!'

The Central Public Works Department people raided these government quarters every day. We came to know that neither the rent nor the electricity charges had been paid for the last ten years. The reason was that 'Tuntun' had been widowed a few years ago, and had thought of nothing except collecting rent for the quarters. Mercifully, the water and power connections of class IV quarters had not been cut off even after non-payment of charges all these years.

Dr. Gurucharan Singh Muhay was insisting on my accompanying them on a visit to Kerala, on LTC. But the children had their exam during that period. I was apprehensive about my wife's reaction to this proposal for a visit to Kerala. But I did go and when I returned after ten days in the south, the people on the ground floor stopped me near the stairs and said, 'The PWD people had come to throw out your luggage–we told them to wait for your return and that you would vacate the house in two days.'

The next day, we put our luggage at a friend's, as a temporary arrangement. Within a week, we had got a room in Sector VIII of R.K. Puram, for which we paid Rs. 5000 as advance. There were very strict conditions attached to the room we rented.

The owner-mistress of this government quarter was running a creche. She would frighten the children she was looking after and force them to go to sleep. She wouldn't allow our children to go out during the day, nor let them speak. She would create problems, 'Bhai sahib, your children are very noisy, your family is also too large. You use too much water for clothes. Vacate the room in a couple of days.'

I recalled what her husband had said a few days earlier, 'Bhai sahib, you wet the whole bathroom–bathe in one corner. You are an educated man.'

My courage seemed to give way under these new developments. It was, perhaps, my fate to worry. I had just paid the children's fees in their new schools, and here I was again homeless only after three months. How much could I go on borrowing? I would think of Bhaia, his determination even in the face of adversities, the money he borrowed, and what he had earned–whatever he had earned had been spent on paying off the loans! It was his courage and grit that had enabled me to go on and I was now earning a good salary.

We both had now decided that we would not get into the vicious circle of renting government quarters. I would have fits of anger, 'The scheduled castes are all allotted government quarters quickly. But I have now been serving for fifteen years–when will I be allotted quarters? When I have only a couple of years left to serve?'

The landlady said, 'Now that you are going, and your luggage is also packed; also it is not raining heavily–it is just a drizzle, and it will go on drizzling like this ...'

Loading our things on to a tempo, we went to the Jain mohalla in Palam village. When our children saw the turds floating in the open sewers, they covered their noses. My wife had fever and she had just entered the room with the children, and had hardly sat down, when the landlady walked in. My wife seemed to be in pain, but the landlady went on talking. Finally, when she did leave my wife told me, 'The old woman was asking me, "what are you, the way people are Brahmins, etc. ..."'

'What did you tell her?' I asked.

'I told her that we were Sikhs. Let us decide what caste we are going to admit to if they ask us again. It should not happen that I tell them one thing and you another.'

We thought about it till midnight. The thought came to us that these people were only bothered about the rent, what do they have to do with our caste? The curse of caste had followed us to the city–though it is said that people living in cities are educated and open-minded!

My wife commented, 'Sesha, who was running the creche, would question me about our caste every now and then, and I used to avoid giving her a direct answer. This old woman has not even let us unload our things and has begun asking about our caste...' She paused and then continued, 'If only Sesha had let the children finish this school session, what difference would it have made? The meters had been disconnected and she was always watering her vegetables and lawn, and yet would always say, "You have a large family... you have three children and I have only two."'

'Do you think she had somehow got a whiff of our caste? Did she not see the name plate outside the door, Gopal Singh Gaur?'

'What can I say about that? But she was always saying that if you are Sikhs then why don't you tie your hair into a bun?'

'The new school is at least a mile from here! Get a cycle, or arrange for a rickshaw for the children to go to school.'

Time and again I would think of what my elder brother had done. Many extended families were living together in these quarters–parents, siblings, and their children. Had we continued living together, it would have been easier to get my fourth sister married.

My wife understood what was gnawing at me mentally. She would say, 'Don't worry about it all the time. It is for children to look after their father's affairs. You should look after your health ... other things will take care of themselves. Go to sleep now.'

This gave me some strength. At least I was not alone and the two of us were together. As the saying goes, 'one and one make eleven!'

In that house of the Jains, at Palam, our policy was to endure what could not be cured. We had to pay the old electricity bill. Even when we had no power in our room, their lights would be burning. I was tired of this recurring problem and one day I said, 'There are a lot of mosquitoes. Let me connect my fan to the switch in your room so that the children might sleep!'

'No, this will mean more load on our connection,' the landlady's daughter-in-law bluntly refused, though they had themselves fixed the electric wires on to the poles, and were actually stealing power.

I had to get up for water sometimes at midnight or early in the morning. Because the pressure was very low it would often take me three hours to collect water. I could not sleep properly, and I felt that my desire to read and write was gradually being overwhelmed by the pressure of all these problems and I felt suffocated... We thought about all these problems deeply, and decided to rent a house nearer to the school.

We now rented a house belonging to B.D. Sharma in Mahavir Enclave in Palam village. He had moved here from Punjab, after selling everything he had owned there, when the militancy had been at its height. Many other businessmen from Amritsar were also living here and carrying on their business. His daughter would often ask my wife about our caste. My wife did not give her a clear answer, 'Perhaps, people cannot digest their food until they are able to verify the caste of others!' she remarked.

One of my colleagues, with whom I had been discussing the difficulties I had been encountering in renting a house suggested, 'You do not wear a turban now, and getting a room on a small rent is an uphill task. Sometimes one has to pretend to be what one actually is not. Listen, one day I was on the terrace of my house in the Jain mohalla, when I saw a man on the adjacent roof. He had a "januo" wrapped round his ear so that all those who saw him may be able to know that he is Brahmin, from a distance. But when I recognized him, I was astonished and asked him, "Purshottam yaar, you? When did you move here? And since when have you become a Brahmin? You had yourself told me that you had been selected on the basis of the quota." His answer was, "Softly please–people asked a thousand questions before renting their rooms and then they would refuse. It was then that I thought of this! I bought a length of thread for a few annas and started wearing it! And now everyone–the Jats and the Jains included, call me 'Panditji ...!'"

'I cannot indulge in this sort of fraud. We must create an awareness against this...But, I cannot pay a high rent!'

'Then, you should be prepared to be evicted every now and then,' he retorted.

The next month, B.D. Sharma suddenly enhanced the rent by three hundred rupees. He imposed another condition, 'If you don't want to pay a higher rent, then put all your three children in my school!'

I spent two weeks looking for another house... One Bihari told me that I had a very large family. Another person from Himachal asked about me and my job, and then pronounced, 'You have been living in Delhi for so many years and are still looking for rented accommodation! Do you have any bad habits ... drinking or ...?'

Many house owners, after making many enquires, would quote an exorbitant rent which was beyond my means.

My wife had a childhood friend who would tell us about houses that were vacant. It was she who had brought us here to this colony. It was through her that we got a dark dingy house on the ground floor in a lane behind her house.

After a couple of days, the landlady, who was from Haryana, asked my wife, 'Are you also Jats like Baljeet (my wife's friend)? They have very large land holdings.'

At that moment, the doorbell rang and Baljeet's children rushed in calling out, 'Masi, Masi', and the landlady went away.

But her investigations did not stop.

'Balbirji, come let's have a drink.' This was the landlord, who was an ex-army man, and when I sat down on the sofa, he said, 'So your house is in the village! In the village, or outside?'

'In the village.' This new trick that he had played on me shook me.

I got up saying, 'I don't drink,' and came away. Who knows what other tricks he would have played on me, had I stayed there.

We stayed for ten months in that house, and then told them that the children had difficulty in negotiating the roads here, and that we had bought a plot on the other side. Now we were about to build our own house.

I saw my wife smiling! Perhaps she had heard my words. We moved our luggage the very next day to the third floor of the new home we had rented.

Within four and a half years this was our sixth house and my eldest daughter's sixth change of school. Every new house meant paying money to new schools. My people in the village would send messages, *you have taken your children and forgotten us. Whenever you think of us, send us some money–otherwise everything is fine. Goodbye.*'

I fretted and fumed, and wondered who was to blame for the predicament that I found myself in! Who was responsible for this? I was worried that these problems would drive me away from my reading and writing–I was now being recognized as a poet. I had won some awards and was now being praised. I didn't want to be distracted from my goal. Such thoughts jostled around in my mind. I reviewed the domestic situation, and devoted myself with greater enthusiasm to translations from Hindi or English into Punjabi. For the first time I sat at a table to do my writing and reading. All along I had worked seated cross-legged on a bed. My waist, back, and legs would begin to ache.

I translated *Lajja* for Arsi Publications, and *Edwina* and *Nehru* for Navyug Publications. While visiting Bhapa Pritam Singh in his office near the Lal Quila, I had often seen starving kids and grown-ups hungrily hunting and licking the leftovers dumped near the street vendors hawking food. I had seen what they called home–the footpath under the open skies. I had also seen their torn, dirty clothes, and mud-spattered feet. All this had left me shaken and deeply moved.

I realized that life was a struggle and there was no escape from it. If I wanted to expand my horizons, I needed to put all the tumult within me into my writings. It hurts me to live in another's house as a tenant, which is a humiliating experience, and an insult and a curse. I wanted to extricate myself from this situation, and longing for the comfort of my own walls, began planning for my own home, which would be my castle.

–Translated by **Tripti Jain**

Notes on Poems

Page 33

1&2. Sahiban-Mirza: Reference to Mirza-Sahiban, a tragic love story popular in Punjab. Mirza, a skilful horseman and archer, and Sahiban, daughter of Siyals of the Khewa village of Jhang district of Punjab, were deeply in love but Sahiban's parents were against their marriage and decided to marry off Sahiban to another man, Tahir Khan. On the day of her wedding, Sahiban eloped with Mirza, both riding on Mirza's mare Bakki. Both of them, out in the open, rested under a Jhand tree. While the tired Mirza slept, Sahiban kept awake watching over him. In the meanwhile, her brothers reached there in search of them. Sahiban, fearing Mirza would shoot her brothers dead with his arrows, hid them, hoping she would be able to convince her brothers not to kill Mirza. But the brothers, the moment they saw Mirza, they shot arrows at him, fatally wounding him. Mirza wanting to retaliate could not find his arrows hidden by Sahiban and died wondering why Sahiban had done this. Sahiban realizing her mistake, killed herself.

Page 34

1. **Farhad**: in Persian literature, a sculptor who was in love with Shirin, a Persian queen. He was asked to carve a staircase up a

mountain if he wanted to marry her, which he did. But he was misled to believe that the queen was dead. Farhad jumped to death from the mountain.

2. **Sutlej-Jamna link canal:** Sutlej Yamuna Link Canal, or SYL as it is popularly known, is a proposed 214-kilometer long canal to connect the Sutlej and Yamuna rivers. Idea is to divide the waters between Punjab and Haryana equitably. The proposal was made in 1956 and the canal remains incomplete because of the dispute on sharing waters between Punjab and Haryana.

Page 36

1. **Eklavya:** A character in Mahabharat. Eklavya was a tribal young man who wanted to learn archery from Guru Dronacharya. Dronacharya refused to be his Guru because he was a Shudra. But, Eklavya determined to become an archer, build a mud idol of Dronacharya and practised archery in front of it and became a skilful archer. When Dronacharya came to know this, he realized that Eklavya had become a better archer than Arjun. Not wanting a Shudra to excel a Kashtriya prince in archery he asked Eklavya to give his right thumb in Gurudakshina. Eklavya readily agreed and cut off his right thumb. But later he learnt to shoot with his left hand and became an equally good archer.
2. **Banda Singh Bahadur**: (1670-1716) One of the great Sikh martyrs. Originally a Jammu Rajput by the name Madho Das, he was converted to Sikh faith by the tenth Sikh Guru Gobind Singh when he met him in Nanded in Maharashtra in 1708. He was a great general and administrator who through his whirlwind conquests against the Mughal armies in Punjab perhaps prepared the ground for the foundation of a Sikh state later by Maharaja Ranjit Singh. Banda was caught by the Mughals and brought to Delhi where he was tortured in a most cruel manner and killed.
3. **Pir Buddhu Shah**: Pir Buddhu Shah (1641-1709) was a Muslim saint who lived at Sadhaura in Himachal Pradesh. He became friendly with Guru Gobind Singh. He helped the Guru in his battle of Bhangani against the hill rajas with his seven hundred

followers. Later when Aurangzeb came to know that he had helped the Guru he had him executed. Banda Singh Bahadur avenged Pir Buddhu Shah's execution in 1709 by storming Sadhaura and punishing Usman Khan. The ancestral house of Pir Buddhu Shah in Sadhaura has since been converted into a Gurdwara named after Pir Buddhu Shah.

4. **Neruda:** Pablo Neruda (1904-73), Nobel Prize winning Chilean poet, diplomat, communist, politician. Wrote in Spanish.

Page 41

1. **Varna System:** Varna, a Sanskrit word with several meanings including type, order, colour or class, is used to refer to social stratification in the Hindu Dharamshastras like the Manusmriti. These and other Hindu texts classified the society into four varnas: Brahmins–priests, scholars and teachers; Kshatriyas–rulers, warriors and administrators; Vaishyas–agriculturalists and merchants; Shudra–labourers and service providers. Communities which belong to one of these four varnas are called **savarna** or "caste Hindus". Dalits and scheduled tribes, who don't belong to the to any varna, are called **avarna**. They are outcastes.

Page 49

1. **Rahu-Ketu:** The mythical demons who are said to devour the moon and the sun and causing the lunar and solar eclipses. Rather, they are the head (Rahu) and headless body (Ketu) of one Danav (demon) named Rahuketu who had drunk Amrita (allotted only to devtas, gods) after Sagarmanthan, (churning of the ocean to discover various treasures, amrita being one of them) by tricking the gods and become immortal. However, he was discovered in the act by gods Moon and Sun and his head was severed from his body by Vishnu, disguised as Mohini, using his Sudarshan Chakra. That explains why the now immortal Rahu-Ketu devour the sun and the moon as a revenge. Here Rahu-Ketu symbolize men of the dominant castes who roam freely out to rape young girls of the lower castes.

Page 50

1. **Belchi and Pipra:** villages in Bihar where a number of Dalit families were burnt alive in 1977

Page 63

1. **Tulsi:** Awadhi (a dialect of Hindi) poet Tulsidas (1532-1623), composer of *Ramcharitmanas*
2. **Manu:** in the Hindu mythology the first man and the creator of Manu-smriti, the Code of Manu, one of the Dharamshastras of Hinduism

Page 71

1. **Ichhran:** one of the two wives of Raja Salwan a north Indian king in 2nd century CE, and mother of Pooran, the other being Loona. Pooran was born to Queen Ichhiran. Upon a suggestion of the astrologers, Pooran was sent away from the King for the first 12 years of his life. It was said that King should not see the face of his son. While Pooran was away, the King married a young girl named Loona. After 12 years of isolation, Pooran returned to the royal palace. There, Loona became romantically attracted towards Pooran. Being a stepson, Pooran disapproved of her advances. A hurt Loona accused Pooran of violating her honor. Pooran was ordered to be amputated and killed. The king's soldiers cut off his hands and legs and threw him into a well in the forest. However, he was rescued and his limbs restored by a Nath sect Guru Gorakhnath and adopted as his disciple and Pooran became a yogi. Sometime later Pooran visited his hometown. King Salwan and Queen Loona came to see him. They did not know his true identity. Pooran asked Salwan about his son. Loona had an emotional breakdown. She was mad with grief for having an innocent boy killed for petty reasons. Pooran forgave his stepmother and father.

Page 74

1. **Bakki:** the mare that belonged to Mirza, in the Mirza-Sahiban love story

Page 78

1&2. **Ichhran and Salwan(s)**: see the reference on page 71

Page 79

1. **Narad(s):** in Hindu mythology, a sage carrier of news and stories, regarded both wise and mischievous
2. **Shakuni(s):** in Mahabharat, Duryodhana's maternal uncle, who helps the Kauravas to cheat the Pandavas in the gambling game in which the Pandavas lose everything

Page 80

1. **Behdas:** homes of the Dalit communities in a Punjab village

Page 81

1. **Sardar:** reference to the Iraqi dictator Saddam Hussain (1937-2006)
2. **Dhantran:** reference to Dhanvantari, the Hindu god of medicine and said to be an avatar of Lord Vishnu. He is mentioned in the Puranas as the god of Ayurveda. Here the crooked politicians are compared to him, ironically, as experts in understanding politics just as Dhanwantri was an expert in medicine.

Page 87

1. **Mirza's Jhand :** The Jhand tree under which Mirza and Sahiban rested after Sahiban had eloped with Mirza.

Page 88

1. **Siyals;** the tribe of the Khewa region, (Jhang districts of Pakistani Punjab). Sahiban was the daughter of the Siyals, just as Heer of another tragic love story Heer-Ranjha was. (also refer to item 1 on page 33)

Page 91

1. **Amur:** The Amur is one of the longest rivers in Asia, flowing thousands of kilometres from the steppes of Mongolia through the untamed wilderness of China and Russia and ending at the Strait of Tartary where it empties into the Pacific Ocean.

Page 98

1. **Koh-e-Qaf:** Mount Qaf in Arabic tradition is a mysterious mountain renowned as the 'farthest point of the earth' owing to its location at the far side of the ocean encircling the earth. It surrounds the earth.

2. **Takhat Hazara:** a town near the river Chenab in the Sargodha district of Punjab in Pakistan. It is the town where Ranjha, the protagonist of the tragic love story of Heer-Ranjha (composed by Waris Shah) lived.

Page 99

1. **Kissa (Qissa):** a form of oral story-telling in Punjabi literature. Most of the stories in the Kissa tradition are about love, passion, betrayal, sacrifice, social values and the common man's revolt against a larger system.

Acknowledgements

First of all, I am thankful to Balbir Madhopuri who offered to have his poetry translated by me. This happened when I met him fortuitously at Punjabi Bhawan, New Delhi when I went there to consult the library for some references while I was translating Lal Singh Dil poetry into English. I am grateful to Prof. Raj Kumar Hans who agreed to write an introduction to this collection of poems. My gratitude is also due to Prof. Raj Kumar, Head of the Department of English, University of Delhi for reading through the manuscript and offering his valuable comments. My thanks are also due to Prof. Raj Kumar and Dr. Renuka Singh of Jawaharlal Nehru University for allowing me to use their comments on Madhopuri's poetry.

I am also thankful to Oxford University Press and Mr. Paritosh Jain, legal heir of Late Dr. Tripti Jain, for permission to use the chapter *Being a Tenant* out of Balbir Madhopuri's autobiography translated by her.

I am specially thankful to my daughter Radha who has produced the cover design for this book as well, as for all my previous books. I also thank Lokesh Karekar for the image on the cover.

I am truly obliged to Rahul Saxena of LG Publishers Distributors for his readiness to publish this book.

—T.C. Ghai